Little People, BIG DREAMS™
FRIDA KAHLO

Written by
Maria Isabel Sánchez Vegara

Illustrated by
Gee Fan Eng

Translated by Emma Martinez

Frances Lincoln
Children's Books

Frida Kahlo was born in Mexico. Just by looking at her you could see she was special.

When she was at school she got very sick.

The illness made her leg as skinny as a rake.

But Frida didn't complain. She was different. She liked to dress differently, too.

Then one day, a bus Frida was riding crashed into a car. Life as she knew it changed forever.

After her accident, Frida had to rest in bed. To help the hours pass, she drew pictures of her foot.

Then, even though she was still in pain, Frida decided to draw self-portraits using a mirror.

Painting by painting, Frida—and her art—got better. It was time to show her pictures to someone else.

She visited the famous artist, Diego Rivera, who couldn't believe his eyes. He wasn't sure what he liked more—her pictures, or her.

Frida and Diego fell in love. They were so similar, and yet so different. But through their ups and downs, Diego encouraged Frida in her paintings.

Through her wonderful pictures, Frida spoke about how she was feeling. In some she looked sad but in others, she smiled.

Eventually Frida decided to show everyone her work. Her pictures caused a great stir in New York City.

When the exhibition came to Mexico, Frida was so sick she had to be in bed. But it was clear that nothing could stop her from painting—not sickness, pain, or heartache.

Frida Kahlo taught the world to wave goodbye to bad things and say "Viva la vida..."

"Live life."

FRIDA KAHLO

(Born 1907 • Died 1954)

1919

1939

Frida Kahlo was born in Coyoacán, a small town outside Mexico City. When she was six, she contracted polio, leaving one leg skinnier than the other. As she grew older, she took part in tomboy activities like riding a bike and playing sports, and once wore male clothes and slicked back her hair for a family photograph. In 1925, Frida was in a bus crash that left her with a lot of painful injuries, including a broken collarbone, ribs, and pelvis. While recovering, instead of continuing her studies, she took up painting—mainly pictures of herself—from her bed.

1942–5 1944

Her husband, the famous Mexican artist Diego Rivera, was a great supporter of her artwork, and in 1938 Frida had her first solo exhibition in New York City. However, Frida only became famous internationally after her death. Her paintings are instantly recognizable because of their bright colors and symbols of Mexican culture, and have been sold for millions of dollars around the world. Thanks to her strong personality, fighting spirit, and love of painting, Frida overcame the accident that marked her life. She is an inspiration to many women today.

Want to find out more about **Frida Kahlo**?
Have a read of these great books:

Who Was Frida Kahlo? by Sarah Fabiny and Jerry Hoare
Frida and Diego: Art, Love, and Life by Catherine Reef
13 Women Artists Children Should Know by Bettina Shuemann
And if you're in Mexico City, you could even visit the house that Frida lived in!
This museum features Frida's outfits, jewelry, and belongings, as well as her art.
www.museofridakahlo.org.mx

Brimming with creative inspiration, how-to projects, and useful information to enrich your everyday life, Quarto Knows is a favourite destination for those pursuing their interests and passions. Visit our site and dig deeper with our books into your area of interest: Quarto Creates, Quarto Cooks, Quarto Homes, Quarto Lives, Quarto Drives, Quarto Explores, Quarto Gifts, or Quarto Kids.

Text copyright © 2014 Maria Isabel Sánchez Vegara. Illustrations copyright © 2014 Gee Fan Eng.
Original concept of the series by Maria Isabel Sánchez Vegara, published by Alba Editorial, s.l.u
Little People, Big Dreams and Pequeña & Grande are registered trademarks of Alba Editorial, s.l.u. for books, printed publications, e-books, and audiobooks. Produced under license from Alba Editorial, s.l.u.

First published in the USA in 2016 by Frances Lincoln Children's Books.

This gift box set edition first published in the USA in 2018 by Frances Lincoln Children's Books
an imprint of The Quarto Group,
100 Cummings Center, Suite 265D, Beverly, MA 01915, USA.
T +1 978-282-9590 F +1 078-283-2742 QuartoKnows.com

First published in Spain in 2014 under the title *Pequeña & Grande Frida Kahlo*
by Alba Editorial, s.l.u.
Baixada de Sant Miquel, 1, 08002 Barcelona www.albaeditorial.es

All rights reserved

No part of this publication may be reproduced, stored in a retrieval system, or transmitted,
in any form, or by any means, electrical, mechanical, photocopying, recording or otherwise without the prior written permission of the publisher.

ISBN: 978-1-78603-428-1

Manufactured in Guangdong, China CC112021

15

Photographic acknowledgments (pages 28-29, from left to right) 1. Photo © FineArt / Alamy 2. Diego Rivera with Wife Frida Kahlo, Photo © Bettmann/CORBIS 3. Frida Kahlo reclining on her bed in Coyoacán, Mexico, between 1942 and 1945, Chester Dale papers, 1897-1971, (bulk 1950-1968), Photo © Archives of American Art, Smithsonian Institution 4. Frida Kahlo © Corbis

Collect the Little People, BIG DREAMS™ series:

FRIDA KAHLO	COCO CHANEL	MAYA ANGELOU	AMELIA EARHART	AGATHA CHRISTIE	MARIE CURIE	ROSA PARKS	AUDREY HEPBURN
EMMELINE PANKHURST	ELLA FITZGERALD	ADA LOVELACE	JANE AUSTEN	GEORGIA O'KEEFFE	HARRIET TUBMAN	ANNE FRANK	MOTHER TERESA
JOSEPHINE BAKER	L. M. MONTGOMERY	JANE GOODALL	SIMONE DE BEAUVOIR	MUHAMMAD ALI	STEPHEN HAWKING	MARIA MONTESSORI	VIVIENNE WESTWOOD
MAHATMA GANDHI	DAVID BOWIE	WILMA RUDOLPH	DOLLY PARTON	BRUCE LEE	RUDOLF NUREYEV	ZAHA HADID	MARY SHELLEY
MARTIN LUTHER KING JR.	DAVID ATTENBOROUGH	ASTRID LINDGREN	EVONNE GOOLAGONG	BOB DYLAN	ALAN TURING	BILLIE JEAN KING	GRETA THUNBERG
JESSE OWENS	JEAN-MICHEL BASQUIAT	ARETHA FRANKLIN	CORAZON AQUINO	PELÉ	ERNEST SHACKLETON	STEVE JOBS	AYRTON SENNA
LOUISE BOURGEOIS	ELTON JOHN	JOHN LENNON	PRINCE	CHARLES DARWIN	CAPTAIN TOM MOORE	HANS CHRISTIAN ANDERSEN	STEVIE WONDER

MEGAN RAPINOE	MARY ANNING	MALALA YOUSAFZAI	ANDY WARHOL	RUPAUL	MICHELLE OBAMA	MINDY KALING	IRIS APFEL

ROSALIND FRANKLIN	RUTH BADER GINSBURG	MARILYN MONROE	KAMALA HARRIS	ALBERT EINSTEIN	CHARLES DICKENS	YOKO ONO	MICHAEL JORDAN

NELSON MANDELA	PABLO PICASSO	AMANDA GORMAN	GLORIA STEINEM	FLORENCE NIGHTINGALE	HARRY HOUDINI	J.R.R. TOLKIEN	

ACTIVITY BOOKS

STICKER ACTIVITY BOOK

COLORING BOOK

LITTLE ME, BIG DREAMS JOURNAL

Discover more about the series at www.littlepeoplebigdreams.com